On The Way With Jesus

Cycle A
Sermons for Lent and Easter
Based on the Gospel Texts

April Yamasaki

CSS Publishing Company, Inc.
Lima, Ohio

ON THE WAY WITH JESUS

FIRST EDITION
Copyright © 2019
by CSS Publishing Co., Inc.

Published by CSS Publishing Company, Inc., Lima, Ohio 45807. All rights reserved. No part of this publication may be reproduced in any manner whatsoever without the prior permission of the publisher, except in the case of brief quotations embodied in critical articles and reviews. Inquiries should be addressed to: CSS Publishing Company, Inc., Permissions Department, 5450 N. Dixie Highway, Lima, Ohio 45807.

Library of Congress Cataloging-in-Publication Data

Names: Yamasaki, April, author. Title: On the way with Jesus : Cycle A sermons for Lent and Easter based on the Gospel texts / April Yamasaki. Description: FIRST EDITION. | Lima : CSS Publishing Company, Inc., 2019. Identifiers: LCCN 2019011503 | ISBN 9780788029936 (pbk. : alk. paper) | ISBN 0788029932 (pbk. : alk. paper) Subjects: LCSH: Lenten sermons. | Jesus Christ--Passion--Sermons. | Eastertide--Sermons. | Bible. Gospels--Sermons. | Church year sermons. | Common lectionary (1992). Year C. Classification. LCC BV4277 Y36 2019 | DDC 252/.62--dc23 LC record available at https://lccn.loc.gov/2019011503

For more information about CSS Publishing Company resources, visit our website at www.csspub.com, email us at csr@csspub.com, or call (800) 241-4056.

e-book:
ISBN-13: 978-0-7880-2994-3
ISBN-10: 0-7880-2994-0

ISBN-13: 978-0-7880-2993-6
ISBN-10: 0-7880-2993-2   PRINTED IN USA

For all travelers

Contents

Preface   7

Ash Wednesday
Matthew 6:1-6, 16-21
With Gratitude And Humility   9

Lent 1
Matthew 4:1-11
In The Wilderness   15

Lent 2
Matthew 17:1-9
On The Mountaintop   21

Lent 3
John 4:5-42
Transformed   27

Lent 4
John 9:1-41
Sent   33

Lent 5
John 11:1-45
When The Way Means Staying Home   39

Liturgy of the Passion/Palm Sunday
Matthew 26:14-27:66
When The Way Is Hard   45

Maundy Thursday
John 13:1-17, 31b-35
The Way Of The Lord   51

Good Friday
John 18:1-19:42
Facing Death 57

Easter Sunday/Resurrection Of Our Lord
Matthew 28:1-10
Forgiven 63

Easter 2
John 20:19-31
With Peace For The Fearful 69

Easter 3
Luke 24:13-35
With Burning Hearts 75

Easter 4
John 10:1-10
With Challenge And Invitation 81

Easter 5
John 14:1-14
The Way For Troubled Hearts 87

Easter 6
John 14:15-21
Framed By Love 93

Easter 7
John 17:1-11
Praying All The Way 99

About The Author 105

Preface

By today's standards, Jesus never traveled far during his earthly ministry, yet he always seemed to be on the move — in the wilderness, along the lakeshore, in the synagogue, to the temple, walking with his disciples, through town and countryside. As an itinerant preacher and teacher, Jesus always seemed to be on the way to or from somewhere.

In this collection of sermons, we follow Jesus on the way to the cross, through the terrible events of his arrest, torture, and execution, to the glorious good news of his resurrection and joyful reunion with his followers, and beyond. We journey through the church year from Ash Wednesday through Lent and the Easter season, moving with the seasons as they change while holding on to the sure hope of God's unchanging love. At the same time, we reflect on our own way through life - our twists and turns through the wilderness, our seasons of doubt and questioning, our times of lament and celebration. Whatever roads we travel, whatever choices we face at the crossroads of life, Jesus leads the way and calls us to follow.

For pastors charged with the responsibility of preaching alongside many other tasks, I offer these sermons as a resource and aid to your preparation. May they inspire and provoke your own thinking as you engage with scripture and seek to serve your congregations. For those interested in personal or small-group study, may these sermons add to your reflection and conversation, and equip you for daily living. For all of us, may we walk in faith and prayer as we travel on the way with Jesus.

– April Yamasaki

Ash Wednesday

Matthew 6:1-6, 16-21

With Gratitude And Humility

On a recent trip out of town, I stayed at a hotel that offered a complimentary breakfast. After serving myself from the generous buffet, I decided to send a photo of my breakfast to my sisters just for fun. I re-arranged the country-fried potatoes on my plate, moved the sausage patty and hard-boiled egg so they were nestled beside the potatoes, with the watermelon and other fresh fruit filling the rest of the plate. With my cup of herbal tea and cutlery to the right, and my newspaper to the upper left, the scene was set. I took the photo, sent it to my sisters, then thoroughly enjoyed my breakfast.

Sending that photo seemed like a quick and easy way to keep in touch while on my trip. But in our selfie world, taking and sharing photos can sometimes get out of hand. "If you don't post a picture, it didn't happen," some say. So we document what we had for breakfast and baby's first steps, a family birthday, an evening with friends, and so much more. Only the pictures we share tend to be carefully arranged to look their best just like my breakfast photo. It's fun, quick, and easy to do. Yet according to "Psychology Today", the cumulative effect of all our carefully curated photos may not be as fun as we compare them with the humdrum of our daily lives. After all, the ordinary, uncurated reality we live every day can never measure up. Some studies suggest that endlessly scrolling through the idealized versions we see on Facebook and Instagram can even lead to depression.

The technology to curate our lives online may be relatively new, but the impulse to re-arrange our lives and show them in the best possible light is an ancient one, dating back to Adam and Eve who dressed themselves in fig leaves to cover up their nakedness. For them too, appearances mattered. But as they discovered when God sought them out in the garden, God's concern was less about their appearance and more about their heart and having authentic relationship.

Jesus made the same point in our scripture reading for today as he addressed the spiritual practices of giving to the poor, praying, and fasting. Today we might need to say if you give to the poor, if you pray, if you fast, but these were such common practices among the religious people of Jesus' day that he said, when you give, when you pray, when you fast. These were three ways that the people expressed their covenant relationship with God, and Jesus' first followers would have been familiar with all three.

Giving was part of regular temple worship—both giving animal sacrifices and giving money in the offering box at the temple entrance. Public festivals provided formal opportunities to give, and there were always the more informal opportunities at the side of the road. In the world of the New Testament, there seemed to be beggars everywhere—those who were blind, lame, or afflicted with some other disease might beg for coins outside the temple or anywhere.

Prayer was a common practice both as a gathered community in the synagogue and temple and more personally. Some prayers were memorized and prayed at certain times of the day, morning, afternoon, and evening. Prayer and fasting came together on national days like the Day of Atonement when all of the people would fast and pray together. The Pharisees also fasted twice a week on a regular basis, on Mondays and Thursdays.

Today we might think of giving, praying, and fasting as three separate and very different forms of spiritual practice, but Jesus understood and addressed them in the same way. When you give, do not give like a hypocrite; instead, give in the way I teach you, and your Father will reward you. When you pray, do not pray like a hypocrite; instead, pray the way I teach you, and your Father will reward you. When you fast, do not fast like a hypocrite; instead fast the way I teach you, and your Father will reward you.

For each practice, Jesus added some provocative details. When you give, don't announce your offering with trumpets to be honored by others. Here he used exaggerated language to make his point: Don't give to draw attention to yourself so that others will see and admire you. In the same way--when you pray, don't stand out in the street so others can see and admire your faithfulness. When you fast, don't look sad and gloomy, so that it's obvious to everyone that you're fasting, so everyone can say how spiritual you are. If you do these things for show, then you already have your reward.

Instead, Jesus taught that when you give, don't even let your left hand know what your right hand is doing. Again, he used exaggerated language to make his point. Don't give in order to be seen. When you pray, instead of praying so other people can see you, pray in secret where God alone is your witness. When you fast, don't look gloomy, but instead wash your face and anoint your head as you would normally do. In other words, don't do these things to impress others. Don't show off.

There are plenty of other reasons to give to the poor, to pray, and to fast. In one survey, some said they give out of compassion for those in need, some because they believe in a cause and want to help, some out of religious obligation, some for a tax break. Prayer can be a way of expressing our faith and connecting with God, and is reported to improve sleep and mental health. I've seen fasting promoted as a weight loss strategy, or as a way of reducing inflammation from arthritis or other conditions. Others see fasting as a religious practice to devote time to prayer.

These may all be good, practical reasons to give, pray, and fast, but Jesus pointed to just one motive and one reward that comes from the Father. Giving is not only about the tax receipt. Praying is not only about getting our prayers answered in the way that we want. Fasting is not only for the physical health benefits. Instead, the reward for giving, praying, and fasting is the reward of a closer relationship with God. That may be why Jesus so often called on God as Father — to highlight the personal and loving relationship we can have with God.

Don't do religious things for show. Give to your local food bank without telling anyone. Take a moment to offer a prayer of gratitude before you get out of bed in the morning and before other people see you. Give up something for Lent without congratulating yourself. Don't be fake. Don't be a hypocrite. Be authentic. "Draw near to God, and he will draw near to you" (James 4:8).

Jesus' teaching about giving, praying, and fasting in secret might seem at odds with Ash Wednesday. After all the sign of the cross on our foreheads is anything but secret.

Ash Wednesday

As ash it's a sign of sorrow, a testimony to the fragility of life like dust, a witness that we are human. Yet the cross also reminds us that joy triumphs over sorrow, that death is not the end, that there is a reality beyond what we can see, smell, hear, taste, and touch.

Like any worship service or spiritual practice or good deed, Ash Wednesday might also become an occasion for pride and showing off. Just as we might give or pray or fast to impress others, we might come to Ash Wednesday with that same tendency to make ourselves look good and give ourselves a pat on the back for taking part. But that would miss the whole point of Ash Wednesday as a solemn remembrance of our human frailty and a time for confession and repentance.

So instead of wearing the sign of the cross proudly as a badge of honor, receive it with gratitude and humility. Receive it in repentance and trust in God's love and forgiveness. Let this outward sign move us to prayer and deepen our faith as we draw near to God.

> *Father in heaven who sees in secret, look kindly on us who gather here. By your mercy, forgive us where we have been quick to draw attention to ourselves, where we have acted more for show than out of sincere faith. With this sign of the cross, remind us of our shared humanity, renew us in authentic relationship with you, and travel with us on the way ahead. Amen.*

Lent 1

Matthew 4:1-11

In The Wilderness

In Hannah Hurnard's classic allegory, *Hinds' Feet on High Places*, little Much-Afraid leaves her home in the Valley to journey to the High Places at the invitation of the Great Shepherd. In the High Places she would finally be delivered from all her fears, her crooked feet made straight, and she would be transformed into Grace and Glory. As she travels, she passes through lovely meadows filled with flowers, over paths where she must clamber over sharp rocks, uphill, downhill, and through the wilderness. Just when she thinks she might begin the final ascent to the High Places, her path turns down or suddenly swings in the opposite direction.

For much of the way, our heroine travels hand-in-hand with two faithful companions named Sorrow and Suffering. In spite of their woeful names, they prove to be help and comfort to her, and in times of great need, Much-Afraid also calls upon the Shepherd. Each time he arrives to reassure her, steady her feet, and lead her onward. After all, the Shepherd knows every step of her way, and he has the added benefit of experience. For the Shepherd had also traveled a road with rough terrain and unexpected turns.

One unexpected turn came to Jesus the shepherd as he was about to begin his earthly ministry. At his baptism, the heavens opened, the Spirit of God descended on him, and a voice from heaven proclaimed, "This is my Son, the beloved, with whom I am well pleased" (Matthew 3:16-17). After such a dramatic introduction, we might imagine Jesus' next step would be addressing the crowds, walking on water, or performing some other miracle. With heaven's endorsement, he could move quickly to begin his mission, to build his platform and reinforce his personal brand as we might say today.

But instead of using his baptism to remain in the public eye, instead of trying to capitalize on the heavenly voice and gain influence among the people, Jesus followed the Spirit's leading into the wilderness. Away from the crowds, he moved into a time of solitude. Away from public acclaim and the relative safety of being part of a group, he was tempted and tried by the devil. The road for Jesus took this unexpected turn--away from immediately growing his ministry to spending time in the wilderness.

Like Much-Afraid — and like Jesus himself — we may find ourselves on an unexpected road. The Spirit may seem to lead us in the opposite direction of our dreams and fervent hopes. Our promising beginning may fall flat, our careful plans may dissolve on us, and we too may find ourselves in an unfamiliar place of wilderness. At those times of testing, we might feel disappointed, discouraged, or afraid, tempted to give up, lost in the wilderness, and wanting desperately to get out. But where is the way forward, and how do we find it?

In his wilderness, Jesus confronted three specific temptations, and each time he responded with the words of scripture. Turn these stones into bread, said the devil, and Jesus replied, "It is written, 'One does not live by bread alone, but by every word that comes from the mouth of God'" (Matthew 4:4). Throw yourself down and let God save you, said the devil, and Jesus replied, "Again

Lent 1

it is written, 'Do not put the Lord your God to the test'" (Matthew 4:7). Worship me and I will give you all the kingdoms of the world, said the devil, and Jesus replied, "Away with you, Satan! for it is written, 'Worship the Lord your God, and serve only him'" (Matthew 4:10).

When life takes an unexpected turn and I suddenly find myself in the wilderness of temptation and trial, I also find strength and courage in the words of scripture. It is written, I remind myself: "Do not fear, for I have redeemed you; I have called you by name, you are mine" (Isaiah 42:1). It is written: "Peace I leave with you; my peace I give to you. I do not give to you as the world gives. Do not let your hearts be troubled, and do not let them be afraid" (John 14:27). It is written: "See what love the Father has given us, that we should be called children of God; and that is what we are" (1 John 3:1).

The words of scripture don't always come to me immediately as they seemed to come at once to Jesus in the wilderness. Some do, thanks to my Sunday school days of memorizing Bible verses and my reading and re-reading of scripture over the years. At other times I search through the bible with the help of my Bible dictionary, concordance, and other study tools. Time in the wilderness means it's time to turn to scripture as Jesus did.

Later in the gospel story, the Pharisees and Sadducees would test Jesus by asking for a sign from heaven (Matthew 16:1). When Jesus told his disciples about his coming suffering, death, and resurrection, Peter protested that this should never happen. It was another test of Jesus' resolve that he answered in the strongest terms: "Get behind me, Satan!" (Matthew 16:23). Even as Jesus hung on the cross, people tempted him with their taunts: "You who would destroy the temple and build it in three days, save yourself! If you are the Son of God, come down from the cross" (Matthew 27:40).

Just as Jesus had faced temptation in the wilderness, he faced temptation and trial throughout his ministry—not always by quoting scripture, but grounded in his identity, mission, and dependence on God. That's why he refused to give the Pharisees and Sadducees an extra sign—his life and ministry were already signs for those with eyes to see. His sense of mission led him to rebuke Peter and to submit to death on a cross, for he knew who he was and where he was going, and "[h]aving loved his own who were in the world, he loved them to the end" (John 13:1).

As Jesus withstood temptation and trial, I am struck by how alone he was. He was alone in the wilderness with the devil. He was alone with the angels to serve him only when the trial was over. He was alone in rebuking the Pharisees and Sadducees, and he was alone in the garden as he struggled in prayer, while his disciples gave into temptation and fell asleep (Mark 14:32-42). At least Much-Afraid had Sorrow and Suffering to keep her company and help her on the way. At least we, as fellow travelers, can encourage one another and share the load.

As Much-Afraid continues her journey to the High Places, she has faith in the Shepherd and in his promise to protect and guide her. Even when the way seems to go in the opposite direction at times, in spite of her doubts and fears, she continues on the way with Jesus. In the end her mission is complete as she reaches the High Places and receives her new name of Grace and Glory. Even her travelling companions are transformed from Suffering and Sorrow to Joy and Peace. Through all of her adventures and mis-adventures, the Good Shepherd remains her consolation and best friend.

Lent 1

And so it is on our way through life. On unexpected pathways and in the wilderness of trial and temptation, we too can trust God to lead us onward. Inspiration and comfort may come to us in the words of scripture, from faithful companions who travel with us, and in our relationship of trust with the shepherd, the guardian of our souls (1 Peter 2:25). Then may we be led out of the wilderness and out of the valley to God's grace and glory, joy and peace.

Great shepherd and guardian, we give thanks for your example in the wilderness, meeting trial and temptation with faith, perseverance, scripture, and wisdom. When life takes an unexpected turn, grant us faith and keep us close to you. In times of temptation, give us courage and perseverance to do what is right. Make us wise to search the scriptures, and in all things to call on you. Amen.

Lent 2
Matthew 17:1-9

On The Mountaintop

Whenever my husband and I see a movie in a theater, we're generally the last to leave. Other movie goers have already gathered up their coats and left the building. An usher stands waiting to pick up any litter and get ready for the next show. But we're still in our seats, savoring the closing music and watching the credits roll. After the big-name stars, we like to see what other names we might recognize, perhaps an actor that we've seen in another film or on TV. I always check to see if April Webster did the casting since she and I share the same name.

I suppose our habit of staying until the very end of a movie reflects the frugality of our days as students. If we're going to hand over our precious dollars to see a movie, we want to enjoy every minute and get our money's worth. But we also don't want to miss anything. At the end of some movies, we've been rewarded with a surprise extra scene that makes the movie even more satisfying or sets up for a sequel. So instead of leaving early, we've learned to linger in case there's more to the story. We stay in our seats as if we're not ready for the movie to end.

I imagine that's how Peter felt on the mountaintop with Jesus. One day Jesus took Peter, James, and John up a mountain where they could be alone, away from the crowds and the other disciples. The three might have guessed something special was in store for them, for the mountains had long been a significant place for their people to meet with God. Moses met with God on Mount Sinai and received the Ten Commandments. Elijah challenged the prophets of Baal on Mount Carmel, and God performed a miracle. Jesus went to a mountain to call his first disciples. He gave the Sermon on the Mount. So too for Peter, James, and John, this mountain became a significant meeting place.

There, Jesus suddenly became transformed—his face and his robe shone so brightly that Peter, James, and John could hardly bear the sight. If that display of glory wasn't enough, Moses and Elijah then appeared, and stood talking with Jesus.

I don't know how the disciples knew the two figures were Moses and Elijah, but together, the two represented the Law and the Prophets, and each had their own mountaintop experiences with God. When Moses came down from Mount Sinai with the Ten Commandments, his face was so bright from the divine encounter that the people were afraid, and Moses had to put a veil over his face to shield them (Exodus 34:29-35). On Mount Carmel, when Elijah prayed for God to come down, God answered with a bright flash of fire (1 Kings 18:36-38). Now here on another mountain, Jesus is transformed with a dazzling bright light.

Perhaps seeing Jesus so transformed was such a glorious vision, such a tremendous experience that Peter didn't want it to end. Maybe he wanted to hold on to this spiritual high drama, to extend it by building three shrines and staying right where he was. Perhaps he thought of the Jewish festival of the booths where people would build shelters outdoors and live in them for seven days. The holiday had started as a harvest festival but it became a reminder of how the people of Israel had wandered in the wilderness as part of their exodus from Egypt. Perhaps Peter meant to honor Jesus, Moses, and Elijah with a festival of booths.

Whatever he may have been thinking, as Jesus, Moses, and Elijah continued their conversation, Peter blurted out: " Lord, it is good for us to be here; if you wish, I will make three dwellings here, one for you, one for Moses, and one for Elijah" (Matthew 17:4). How like Peter to have a sudden thought and share it immediately, no matter who else he might be interrupting!

But then it was Peter's turn to be interrupted. For while he was still speaking, God's voice from heaven declared, "This is my Son, the beloved; with him I am well pleased; listen to him!" (Matthew 17:5).

Overwhelmed by fear, the three disciples fell to the ground until Jesus touched them and reassured them: "Get up and do not be afraid" (Matthew 17:7). The voice from heaven was now silent, Moses and Elijah had disappeared, and Jesus led them down the mountain. The disciples were still in awe and confused by what had happened, and Jesus cautioned them not to speak of their experience until after he had been raised from the dead. Then they would understand.

Once down from the mountain and immediately after our text, Jesus and his disciples found themselves again in the midst of a crowd. A boy was suffering with convulsions, and his father pleaded for help. Others milled around, confused and not knowing what to do. The chaotic scene may have prompted Peter to long once again for the solitude of the mountaintop. But Jesus had come not only for his three disciples, but for the crowds, not only for the mountaintop experiences of life, but for those times of confusion and desperation that are also part of human life.

When Peter later described this mountaintop experience in a church letter, he skipped over his own impulsive contribution to the scene to highlight instead the main elements centered on Jesus. The apostle said, "we had been eye witnesses of his majesty" (2 Peter 1:16). Peter, James, and John had seen Jesus bathed in glorious light, and they had heard God's voice of affirmation. In his letter, Peter sought to pass on the good news: "You will do well to be attentive to this as to a lamp shining in a dark place, until the day dawns and the morning star rises in your hearts" (2 Peter 1:19). In other words, Peter said, "Listen!"

Perhaps you've experienced a literal mountaintop in your life, like taking a long, hard hike up a mountain to a breath-taking view of the valley and trees below. Or your mountaintop may have been less literal, like finally completing a tough assignment at work. Perhaps it was the love and beauty of your wedding day or a soaring time of worship. Perhaps it was the birth of a grandchild. You may have wanted to hold on to the excitement and emotional high of your experience - to stay on that mountaintop, so to speak, just like Peter.

But listen to Jesus who said, "Get up and don't be afraid." Mountaintop experiences and emotions don't last forever. A real world is waiting and clamoring for attention. Someone needs a touch of compassion. Someone needs a word of healing. That's what Jesus and his disciples found when they went down from the mountain. We will find that also, and we can carry the lesson of the mountaintop with us: Listen to Jesus.

We can't stay on the mountaintop forever. Nor can we personally meet every need that's part of our clamoring world today. But we can listen to Jesus. Listen deeply

Lent 2

beyond the noise and confusion of yet another phone call, another email, another text message, another ad, another celebrity. We live in an age of information overload with so many different voices calling us in so many different directions. Listening can be overwhelming. Yet God's voice proclaims Jesus, and says, "Listen to him!" Who are the people and the concerns that Jesus has placed in our path today? Listen to Jesus. Get up and don't be afraid.

Lord Jesus, thank you for the mountaintop experiences of life — for moments of joy and deep blessing, and for the glimpses of glory on our way. Thank you for your presence also in the valleys — in times of confusion and great need. In all of life, help us to listen for your voice. Lift our fears. Strengthen our resolve. So may we get up and follow you. Amen.

Lent 3

John 4:5-42

Transformed

In the Orthodox Christian Church, the woman at the well in John's gospel is remembered as Saint Photini, which means "the enlightened one." Apparently her passion for sharing Jesus as the Messiah sent from God did not end with the people of her own town. Instead, church tradition recounts her travels as an evangelist to the city of Carthage in northern Africa and then to the city of Rome where she sought an audience with the emperor Nero. While the emperor agreed to see her, he rebuffed her attempts to convert him, imprisoned her along with her five sisters and younger son who were traveling with her, and subjected them all to cruel tortures. After three years in prison, the others were beheaded, and soon after Saint Photini also gave up her life as a martyr for the Christian faith.

Long before she became Saint Photini, this remarkable woman was the unnamed woman at the well in our text for today. Unlike other women of her time and in her town, she was on her way to draw water at noon. The other women would have come to the well hours before while it was still relatively cool. What's more, they would have most likely come together, for a chance to talk and to help each other hoist their heavy water jugs. But this woman came alone in the heat of the day, as if to avoid the other women. Perhaps she had already been the subject of their gossip and had grown weary of their sidelong glances. Even Jesus apparently knew that she had been married five times and was living with a man who was not her husband.

As the woman made her way toward the well, she could see Jesus sitting by it. By tradition and local custom, Jesus would normally have withdrawn so she would not have to encounter him directly. Their eyes should not meet. They were not to speak to one another. A rabbi would not even speak to his own wife in public, much less a strange woman. A Jew would not speak to a Samaritan, or share a drink out of the same vessel. Most Jews would have taken a different route to avoid traveling through Samaria.

But Jesus was like no one else. He did not move away, and instead of remaining silent, he asked the woman for a drink, and continued to engage her in conversation. He spoke of the gift of God, of living water, and eternal life. He told her to call her husband, then come back, and when she said she had no husband, he somehow knew about her circumstances. Whether she had actually been divorced five times, or been widowed, remains unknown. Just living with a man without being married was scandal enough, yet that didn't stop Jesus from continuing their conversation. He went on to talk with her about worshiping God in the Spirit and in truth.

For her part, the woman was bold enough to question Jesus. She was well aware of the separation between Jews and Samaritans, between men and women, so how then could Jesus ask her for a drink? And where could she get the living water so she would never have to come to the well again? Was this strange man greater than the ancestors who dug this well and those who had used it for generations? Finally, the woman had to ask herself the biggest question of all: Could this man possibly be the long-awaited Messiah?

After her encounter with Jesus, the woman rushed back to the town to tell everyone about Jesus. She left the well in such a hurry that she returned without the water she had come for, and without her water jar. Instead of avoiding others, she now urged everyone to join her: "Come and see a man who told me everything I have ever done! He cannot be the Messiah, can he?" (John 4:29).

Some were ready to believe on the basis of the woman's testimony. Others exercised more caution, but were at least intrigued enough to find out more. They came to meet Jesus for themselves, invited him to stay, and after two more days, they also became convinced. "It is no longer because of what you said that we believe, for we have heard for ourselves," they said, "and we know that this is truly the Savior of the world" (John 4:42). They scarcely gave the woman credit, yet without her testimony, they might never have come to faith. For this, she has often been called the first evangelist and equal to the apostles.

After this account in the gospel of John, the woman disappears from the New Testament record. But clearly she had become an "enlightened" one in keeping with the name she would later receive as Saint Photini. Her ordinary, everyday trip to the well had led to an extraordinary encounter with Jesus that transformed her life. From there she carried his light to her townspeople and beyond. The traditions surrounding her later witness and martyrdom shine with faith and courage.

The interaction between Jesus and the woman at the well has much to teach us about how to reach out to people who are different from us, how to talk with strangers from other faith backgrounds, from other cultures, across gender. Instead of allowing such differences to keep us apart, this text opens up new possibilities for how we might relate to one another. That both Jesus and the woman came to the well in need of water demonstrated their common humanity. Instead of beginning with a sermon, Jesus asked the woman for a drink in a gesture of humility and genuine need. Instead of recoiling from the boldness of this stranger, the woman responded with curiosity and honest questions. They spoke as equals and with respect for one another.

In our world today with its deep divisions and often polarized responses to current events, we need these same qualities: a recognition of our common humanity and our common needs, a posture of humility and honest curiosity, a respect for one another whether or not we share the same background, perspectives, and opinions. The encounter between Jesus and the Samaritan woman offers us a model for reaching across the divides of our own day, for transforming human relationships.

At the same time, this story speaks of personal healing and transformation. As the woman spoke with Jesus, her initial wariness turned to honest engagement. Her honest engagement became a questioning faith. And even though some questions still lingered, she knew enough about Jesus to share with the people in her town. The woman who had come to the well alone in the middle of the day became an evangelist to everyone who would listen. Whatever her past history with her five husbands, whatever her current live-in arrangement, she now had a new relationship with Jesus and a new purpose. God's living water was welling up in her to new life.

Lent 3

For us too, whatever our past and present situation, whatever choices we've had to make in our lives, we too can be transformed. We can live a new life. For by God's grace and power, we are being transformed. Like the woman at the well, we too can receive living water; we can learn to ask new questions, we can grow in faith. We might not evangelize our whole town or die a martyr's death, but we too can share what we know.

Dear Jesus, when the disciples saw you talking with the Samaritan woman, they hardly knew what to say. And when she turned out to be such an effective witness for you, they must have been more astonished still. They had gone to the town in search of food. She had returned to the town to tell everyone about you. We confess that we are often more like the disciples, hardly knowing what to say. In prayer, in personal interactions, with people we know and those who are strangers, make us eager to share. Revive our curiosity, and renew our energy to be faithful witnesses to you. Be our living water welling up in us. Amen.

Lent 4

John 9:1-41

Sent

Last week a friend sent me a copy of her recently released book. When I opened the outer package that gave my address, I discovered another layer of wrapping, this time brown craft paper adorned with a golden leaf and a brief handwritten message in green ink. On the back, a sticker matching her book cover completed the package. Her book was so beautifully presented that I hesitated to unwrap it further, but when I did, I discovered another heartfelt and handwritten message on the book's inside cover. Clearly she had sent this gift with great care and thoughtfulness, attending to every detail, with a sense of purpose.

In today's reading Jesus spoke of God as the one who sent him (John 9:4), and he described himself this way repeatedly throughout the gospel of John. When his disciples brought him something to eat, Jesus said, "My food is to do the will of him who sent me and to complete his work" (John 4:34). When the crowds asked about doing the work of God, Jesus answered, "This is the work of God, that you believe in him whom he has sent" (John 6:29). When there were questions about his teaching, Jesus insisted, "My teaching is not mine but his who sent me" (John 7:16).

The word "sent" carries a special significance, for it means being sent with a purpose. So just before Jesus entered Jerusalem, when he sent two of his disciples ahead, he did so with the purpose that they would make arrangements for him (Mark 11:1). The early church in Jerusalem chose several members and sent them with Paul and Barnabas to Antioch with the purpose of meeting with the Gentile Christians (Acts 15:22). The apostle Paul wrote to the Philippians, "I hope in the Lord Jesus to send Timothy to you soon, so that I may be cheered by news of you" (Philippians 2:19). So too, Jesus was sent by God with a purpose—carefully, thoughtfully, with attention to detail, as a gift for the world--to do God's work, to teach, to preach, to heal, to show the world who God was and is.

    The word "sent" appears twice in our text today: first in Jesus' description of himself as sent by God (John 9:4), and then again in the name of the pool of Siloam which means "Sent." So when Jesus met the man who was born blind, when he made mud and smeared it on the man's eyes, when he sent the man to wash in a pool that just happens to be called "Sent," we might wonder at the significance of their encounter. If being sent means being sent with a purpose, what is the purpose here?

    When Jesus and his disciples first saw the man at the side of the road, the disciples assumed that his blindness was the result of some sin, either his own or his parents. But Jesus said, "Neither this man nor his parents sinned; he was born blind so that God's works might be revealed in him" (John 9:3). As events unfolded, this proved to be the larger purpose at work, for the man dutifully washed his eyes in the pool, received his sight, and by the end of the chapter he came to believe and worship Jesus (John 9:38). God's miraculous work of healing both physically and spiritually had become evident in his life. What a wonderful purpose!

Lent 4

Yet I wonder if everything had felt so wonderful in the moment. Imagine a stranger spitting in the dirt, smearing the mud on your eyes, and telling you to go wash. Would you and I have cooperated so readily? Or would we have recoiled from such an encounter, told the stranger to keep his hands and his saliva to himself? Would we have been offended and turned away, and so missed being healed?

Centuries earlier, an army commander who served the king of Aram had been afflicted with leprosy. When the commander appealed to the prophet Elisha for a cure, the prophet sent him a message to go wash in the Jordan River seven times, and he would be restored to health. But instead of following the prophet's instructions, the commander grew angry. He had expected to meet the prophet personally and to be cured immediately at his word. And why should he wash in the Jordan River when there were many other rivers? He was about to turn away in disgust, when his servants prevailed upon him: "Father, if the prophet had commanded you to do something difficult, would you not have done it? How much more, when all he said to you was, 'Wash, and be clean'?" (2 Kings 5:13). The commander relented, did just as the prophet said, and he was cured of his leprosy.

When the commander was told to go wash, he scoffed at the idea as if it were beneath him. But once he got over his anger, once he washed in the Jordan River and miraculously recovered from his disease, he came to a new understanding and a new faith. "Now I know that there is no God in all the earth except in Israel," he said (2 Kings 5:15). For the blind man too, washing his eyes in a nearby pool might have seemed a trivial and useless exercise. But by sending him to the pool, Jesus started the man on a longer journey of healing, beginning with the recovery of his eyesight and bringing him to faith in Jesus.

Of course, there were challenges along the way. The man's neighbors and people who had seen him at the side of the road couldn't quite believe he was the same man. The Pharisees first questioned him, and when they weren't satisfied, they questioned his parents. Then they questioned the man again. In spite of the questions—or maybe because of them?--his faith continued to grow, he came to know and believe in Jesus, and worshiped him.

For us today, what is the work that we have been sent to do? What is the special purpose that lies before us? Like the army commander, perhaps we expect some great mission. We're ready to march in to battle. We're looking for a challenge. We want to make a difference. We at least want a prophet to come look us in the face.

But perhaps what lies before us this week is considerably more mundane: wiping noses, filling out forms, handling complaints, perhaps another meeting. Maybe it is another pot to scrub or another exam to write, the stuff of ordinary life is whatever that looks like for you. Such small things may seem so insignificant. We may feel frustrated, disappointed, or even angry at their smallness. Surely we were made for something more, we protest.

And yes, we have a larger purpose! Like the blind man in our text, our lives are meant to show the work of God in our lives. Like him, we are sent into our everyday home and family life, and into our work-a-day world with a purpose. Our more immediate tasks may seem laughably simple and small - go wash in the pool, go to school, get to work, do the next to-do on your too-long to-do list, or whatever else has been placed before you this week. But God works in such small things today just as he did for the man who washed in the pool and received his sight. Like him, we have a larger purpose and a longer journey of faith and healing.

So like the blind man who received his sight, let's begin where we are and take that journey that leads to praise and worship and glory to God.

Son of God and Son of man, teacher and healer, open our eyes, enlarge our vision to catch a glimpse of your glory. You are the one sent from God, and you send us with a purpose. May your healing grow in us and make us whole. May your call deepen us and draw us close to you. Then may God's work be evident in and through us. Lord, we believe, and worship you. Amen.

Lent 5

John 11:1-45

When The Way Means Staying Home

A fellow pastor once remarked that a church in our city would need to grow by ten to fifteen percent a year just to stay the same size. His evidence was clearly anecdotal without any survey data or other numbers to back up his comment, but I understood his point. People move from church to church and across denominations. Some people fall ill and become unable to attend as regularly. Some pass from this life to the next. There's movement in and out of our busy urban and suburban area.

One family from our congregation relocated to another town to be part of a Bible study group that they pray will grow into a church. Another family spent some years in overseas ministry, and have now moved to a nearby community to take on pastoral responsibilities. Several young adults are away at school. As much as I would love for them all to remain as part of the congregation, I know that God is calling them elsewhere at least for now.

In response to the call of Jesus, Peter and Andrew left their fishing nets. The sons of Zebedee left their father with the family fishing business. Matthew left his tax collector booth. Women traveled with Jesus and supported him out of their funds. Crowds flocked to hear him teach and followed him even when he tried to get away for some much needed solitude after the death of John the Baptist.

But not everyone who followed Jesus left their homes to follow him around the countryside. In fact, one man who had been healed by Jesus wanted to go with him as a disciple, but Jesus refused. Instead, Jesus told him, "Go home to your friends, and tell them how much the Lord has done for you, and what mercy he has shown you" (Mark 5:19). Others too who had been healed by Jesus returned to their homes: the woman healed of her chronic bleeding, the widow's son raised from the dead, the centurion and his servant healed by Jesus, and many more who had been crippled or blind or suffering from disease. For them, following Jesus meant returning home, staying put, and living faithfully where they were.

In the early church, Christians were known as people of the way (Acts 9:2, 22:4), but that didn't always mean leaving home. Following Jesus was a way of life, whether physically on the road, or at home with family and friends. So also today, some of us may have moved around, some of us may have led a more settled life, but all of us can be on the way with Jesus wherever we are.

Our scripture reading today tells the story of three followers of Jesus whose way meant staying at home. Martha lived with her sister, Mary, and her brother, Lazarus, in the village of Bethany, just a few miles outside of Jerusalem. As a frequent visitor to Bethany, Jesus would often see Martha, Mary, and Lazarus, so when Lazarus became ill, the sisters sent a message to Jesus. Instead of rushing to them immediately, however, Jesus stayed where he was for another two days. By the time Jesus arrived in Bethany, Lazarus had already died.

Martha immediately ran out to meet Jesus, and said, "Lord, if you had been here, my brother would not have died" (verse 21). Their friendship was close enough that she spoke the words of reproach frankly out of her grief. When Mary joined them, she too said the same thing: "Lord, if you had been here, my brother would not have died" (verse 32). Perhaps this had been the sisters' sad refrain over the last few days as they waited for Jesus, then as they mourned and buried their brother: if only Jesus had been here.

When Jesus at last arrived, he went to the tomb with Martha, Mary, and those who were with them. The women had already been crying for days, and Jesus too began to weep. "See how he loved him," murmured the people around him (verse 36). Then Jesus told them to remove the stone. He raised his eyes to heaven and prayed to God, then looked again toward the tomb and cried, "Lazarus, come out!" (verse 43). A figure still wrapped in grave cloths emerged into the light. The people could hardly believe their eyes--Jesus had raised Lazarus from the dead!

How they must have celebrated! Their tears of mourning became tears of joy and laughter. They helped Lazarus remove his bindings, for he was now free from the tomb and free from death. Earlier, Martha had privately said to Jesus that she knew Lazarus would rise again in the resurrection "on the last day" (verse 24), but she had no idea Jesus would raise him on that very day. Jesus was truly "the resurrection and the life" just as he said (verse 25).

In the days after raising Lazarus, Jesus was again on the road preaching, teaching, and healing, and he again was a frequent visitor in Bethany. Martha, Mary, and Lazarus remained at home and continued to host Jesus and his disciples. I imagine Martha welcoming people at the door and hurriedly bringing out more food whenever

Jesus and his disciples arrived. Mary listened attentively to Jesus' teaching. Lazarus might have leaned in close as he too listened to Jesus.

One time Mary anointed Jesus with perfume and wiped his feet with her hair.

On his triumphal entry into Jerusalem, Jesus stopped at Bethany and sent two of his disciples into Jerusalem to get the colt that he would ride, and after his entry into the temple, he and his disciples returned to Bethany for overnight. At his ascension, Jesus again led his disciples out to Bethany.

For Jesus, Bethany played a significant role in his ministry, for there he raised Lazarus from the dead and healed Simon from leprosy. Bethany was a place of preparation before his entry into Jerusalem and before his ascension. The home of Lazarus, Martha, and Mary was a place of hospitality, rest, and friendship for Jesus and his disciples like no other place mentioned in the gospels. No wonder author and speaker Frank Viola calls Bethany "God's favorite place on earth."

What if our homes could play that same kind of role? Could my home and your home also be places of healing where griefs and joys are shared? Could our homes be places where people might say "look how they love one another" and where we could celebrate the life-giving power of God together? Could our homes be places of hospitality and friendship, of preparation for ministry and rest for the weary? What a beautiful vision for home and family life!

It also seems quite impossible, doesn't it? Especially for those of us who may feel weary and in need of someone else to prepare an oasis of rest for us. But as Martha, Mary, and Lazarus found, the presence and prayer of Jesus made all the difference. Without Jesus, Lazarus was dead. But by the power of God, Jesus raised Lazarus from the dead, turning grief into joy, death into life.

Perhaps we could make a start as Martha did, who turned to Jesus with a troubled heart when Lazarus fell ill, and who ran to Jesus when he finally arrived. Like Martha, may we who are weary or grieving or troubled, run to Jesus. May we rest assured that he weeps with us and loves us. May we be at home with him and look to him in confidence as Martha did. Then may God also work a miracle and breathe in us new life.

> *Yours is the resurrection and the life, O God, so renew us by your Spirit. Whether your call takes us on the road or roots us close to home, may we follow your will and way wherever we are. Like Martha, Mary, and Lazarus, may we open our homes and our hearts to Jesus. Then grow us also in offering hospitality and refreshment to others for his sake. Amen.*

Liturgy of the Passion/Palm Sunday
Matthew 26:14-27:66

When The Way Is Hard

In the gospel of Matthew, the sweep of events from Judas' decision to betray Jesus, through his arrest, trial, crucifixion, and burial takes less than fifteen minutes to read aloud. Yet the emotional intensity of these events makes for an exhausting read. Alone in my room, I could hardly make it through. If I were to read this as part of worship in my church, I'd want to skip the regular sermon and plan some silence to reflect and recover before we'd sing a song of response.

Just imagine living and dying through it all. Imagine the agony of Jesus praying alone in the garden, betrayed by one of his closest friends and followers and deserted by the rest. Imagine being arrested and interrogated, spat upon and slapped, then questioned again and again. Imagine being mocked, beaten, and stripped. Each blow and insult was an indignity and a foretaste of death until Jesus' final suffering on the cross and his last breath.

Jesus knew all of that was coming. Well before his arrest, he told his disciples of the suffering and death that awaited him: after Peter's declaration of Jesus as the Messiah (16:13-23), as they gathered in Galilee (17:22-23), and on their way to Jerusalem (20:17-19). Each time Jesus predicted his death — and each time he also told his disciples that he would be raised on the third day. None of that seemed to register with the disciples, not the prediction of his death, nor the resurrection that would follow. But clearly for Jesus, his death and his resurrection were two parts of the same whole, for he spoke of them together, almost in the same breath.

In our text for today, as Matthew retells Jesus' suffering and death, the gospel also includes a number of references to Jesus' coming resurrection. As I read this, I found myself holding on to these points of reassurance and relief in the midst of the horror. For much as Jesus spoke of his death and resurrection together, so the gospel writer describes Jesus' suffering and death with glimpses of resurrection along the way.

Our text begins with Judas agreeing to betray Jesus. Then sandwiched between these opening verses and Jesus' prediction of Peter's denial, Jesus shared one last meal with his disciples. The meal itself was filled with foreboding as Jesus predicted that one of the disciples would betray him, and the bread and cup foreshadowed his broken body and his life poured out in death. But there was also a hint of something more as Jesus said to them, "I tell you, I will never again drink of this fruit of the vine until that day when I drink it new with you in my Father's kingdom" (verse 29). The day would come for them to share another meal together in the Father's kingdom. In the midst of betrayal, denial, and the threat of death, there is this glimpse of resurrection.

In the next few verses, Jesus predicted that all of the disciples would fall away. When Peter protested and insisted that he would remain faithful, Jesus said that before the night was over, Peter would deny him three times. Again Peter protested and the others joined in so vigorously that they missed what Jesus said next: "after I am raised up, I will go ahead of you to Galilee" (verse 32).

Liturgy Of The Passion / Palm Sunday

Denial, desertion, and death will not have the last word, for Jesus will rise again! Another glimpse of resurrection.

Once Jesus was arrested, he was taken before the religious authorities. When he was questioned by the high priest, Jesus said, "From now on you will see the Son of Man seated at the right hand of power and coming on the clouds of heaven" (verse 64). With these words, Jesus clearly testified that his arrest would not be the end. No earthly authority could match his own authority at the right hand of the all-powerful. One day he would rise from death and ascend into heaven. Another glimpse of resurrection.

The only witnesses that could be found to testify against Jesus merely repeated his earlier claim, "I am able to destroy the temple of God and to build it in three days" (verse 61). This was no blasphemy against the temple, for Jesus had been speaking of his body as the temple of God that would be destroyed by his death, and then rebuilt—resurrected—in three days (John 2:18-22). Those who passed by as Jesus hung on the cross clearly understood that he had been referring to his own body, for they taunted him, "You who would destroy the temple and build it in three days, save yourself!" (verse 40). The religious leaders referred to this saying again when they insisted on posting a guard at Jesus' tomb (verses 62-66). As part of the gospel narrative, these references remind us that resurrection is indeed coming. More glimpses of resurrection.

The most explicit reference comes immediately after Jesus' death. The curtain of the temple is torn, and many graves are re-opened as the result of a violent earthquake. Some of the dead are raised just as Jesus had raised Lazarus, and the gospel says that those who were raised would later go into the city "after his resurrection" (verse 53). It seems more fantasy and science fiction than anything else, but whatever we are to make of this part of the story, it too gives another glimpse of resurrection.

Throughout our text, Jesus' innocence is clear. No witnesses gave testimony sufficient to condemn Jesus to death. Pilate found no reason to sentence Jesus to be crucified, and when he asked the crowd, "[W]hat evil has he done?" (verse 23), the crowd only continued to shout for Jesus' death. Pilate washed his hands to demonstrate his innocence of any wrongdoing, at the same time he condemned the innocent Jesus to death. Even Pilate's wife called Jesus "that innocent man" (verse 19). Crucifixion was a cruel death, and the crucifixion of an innocent man even more inhumane and unjust.

Yet in the face of such cruelty and pain, God's good news could not be contained: Jesus who suffered and died arose from the dead! Glimpses of resurrection continually broke through the narrative of denial, betrayal, suffering, and death. Vindicated by God, Jesus was finally raised three days later. Life conquered death. Joy overtook sorrow. Love covered the multitude of our sins. God's power was and is all in all.

The death and resurrection of Jesus is good news for all of us. By the grace of God, we have forgiveness from sin. By the power of his Spirit, we can live a new life. The risen Christ reigns at the right hand of power. Our God is the God of resurrection, and resurrection will break out even at the darkest and most unexpected times.

If you're facing down injustice, if you've been betrayed by someone close to you, if you feel deserted by your friends, know that Jesus has been there too, and is with

Liturgy Of The Passion / Palm Sunday

you now. Hang on to hope. Be steadfast in your testimony. Even when the way is hard - especially when the way is hard - look for signs of resurrection to break out around you.

If you're suffering from physical, mental, emotional, or spiritual pain, if you're facing death as we all must one day, if the humiliation and dread of the coming end looms over you, know that Jesus has been there too, and is with you now. God holds you in the palm of his hand. Good triumphs over evil. Life has conquered death. Resurrection is coming.

> *We give thanks to you, God almighty, for the life, death, and resurrection of Jesus. So much of this story remains a mystery to us—how you could become human in Jesus Christ, who lived, suffered, and died such a cruel death, and then rose again with new life. The earth shook in response, yet the death and resurrection of Jesus form the sure foundation of our faith. We believe. Help our unbelief. We wait for resurrection. Amen.*

Maundy Thursday
John 13:1-17, 31b-35

The Way Of The Lord

For Lent, one year, our worship committee planned to focus on a different name or title given to Jesus in scripture. When we read the story of Nicodemus, I was immediately drawn to Jesus as Savior, sent by God not to judge the world, but to save it. For Jesus' triumphal entry into Jerusalem on Palm Sunday, my sermon highlighted Jesus as king. When it came to the story of Jesus washing the disciples' feet, I first thought of Jesus as servant.

That's definitely part of our reading for today, which tells the story of Jesus serving his disciples by washing their feet. In the world of the New Testament, foot washing was a daily practice. In that warm climate with the dusty dirt roads and dusty dirt pathways, where people wore sandals - without socks - it was customary for people to wash their feet whenever they entered a home, whether their own or someone else's.

It was surprising - maybe even shocking - that Jesus, as the leader of the group, would wash his disciples' feet. Leadership meant taking charge, not washing feet. Leadership meant giving orders, not kneeling down to serve others. Foot washing was a lowly task left mainly to servants. So yes, in this text, there is good reason to think immediately of Jesus as servant.

But that's not how the reading starts. Instead of moving too quickly to Jesus as servant, our reading begins with Jesus as Lord. At the start of John 13, "Jesus knew that his hour had come to depart from this world and go to the Father" (verse 1), and he knew "that the Father had given all things into his hands" (verse 3). Jesus knew he was the Lord with all things under his power. But instead of acting like some kind of celebrity and announcing his power with flashing lights and fireworks, Jesus washed his disciples' feet to demonstrate what it meant for him to be Lord. This is the kind of Lord that Jesus was and is - not the one who lords it over his followers by trying to look and act superior. Instead, we might say that Jesus lords it under them.

Peter was so shocked that he blurted out, "Lord, are you going to wash my feet?" (verse 6). In the absence of servants, Peter would have expected to wash his own feet. In a group of disciples with their Teacher, one of the disciples might have washed Jesus' feet. But how unseemly for the teacher and Lord of the group to wash everybody else's feet!

Peter protested even more strongly: "You will never wash my feet" (verse 8). The force of the original Greek language here is conveyed by the New Living Translation: "you will never ever wash my feet!"

Jesus responded to Peter just as forcefully: "Unless I wash you, you will have no share with me" (verse 8). One day Peter would understand, but for now, he seemed satisfied to take Jesus at his word: "Lord, not my feet only but also my hands and my head!" (verse 9).

Peter wanted to belong to Jesus. Often impetuous, head-strong, talking before anyone else, interrupting even Jesus' conversation with Moses and Elijah on the mountain top, Peter was a rushing-in-where-angels-fear-to-tread kind of guy. But when it came to following Jesus,

Maundy Thursday

Peter was all in. His later denial of Jesus would be all that more devastating, perhaps most of all to himself. At this point, Peter wanted to be completely covered.

Once again, Jesus corrected him: "One who has bathed does not need to wash, except for the feet, but is entirely clean. And you are clean, though not all of you" (verse 10). Jesus knew that Judas would betray him, yet still he washed the feet of Judas. Jesus knew that Peter would later deny him, yet still he washed Peter's feet. He washed the feet of all the disciples even though he knew they would fall asleep when he asked them to keep watch, and they would all flee when he was arrested.

The gospel of John notes that Jesus "[h]aving loved his own who were in the world, he loved them to the end" (verse 1). There's a double meaning here. How long did Jesus love his disciples? He loved them to the end — all the way to the cross, all the way to the end of his life and beyond. And in what way did Jesus love his disciples? He loved them to the end, or to the highest degree possible. *I love you, and I wash your feet, even though you betray me and deny me and run away and leave me to die alone.* That's the great extent of Jesus' love for his disciples, and the great extent of God's love for us.

Our reading describes how Jesus "got up from the table, took off his outer robe, and tied a towel around himself" (verse 4). We might almost skip over these practical details, assuming that Jesus removed his outer robe and wrapped a towel around him, so he wouldn't get his robe wet or dirty. But the word choice here is literally that Jesus "laid aside" his robe, and this same expression is used repeatedly when Jesus speaks about his coming death. "I am the good shepherd," said Jesus, "The good shepherd lays down his life for the sheep" (John 10:11). "I lay down my life for the sheep" (John 10:15), "I lay down my life in order to take it up again" (John 10:17). "No one takes it from me, but I lay it down of my own accord. I have power to lay it down, and I have power to take it up again." (John 10:18). "No one has greater love than this, to lay down one's life for one's friends" (John 15:13).

This similarity in wording between Jesus' laying aside his outer robe and laying down his life connected the two acts. Jesus washing his disciples' feet was a sign of his coming death. So when Peter protested, "You will never wash my feet," it was as if he refused to accept Jesus' death. Peter seemed offended by the very idea that his teacher and lord would wash his feet. In much the same way, today some might be offended by the very idea of Jesus dying on a cross. How un-lord-like. How gruesome. How repulsive. We'd rather think of Jesus teaching or preaching or performing miracles or even serving, instead of dying.

But Jesus said to Peter, "Unless I wash you, you will have no share with me." As a disciple of Jesus, Peter needed to accept Jesus washing his feet, and he needed to accept his death too. Accepting Jesus' death is part of what it means for Jesus to be Lord: the one who saves us from sin and makes us clean, the one who transforms our lives. Peter didn't get it at first. He wasn't willing to accept Jesus as that kind of Lord in his life. He protested. He didn't want Jesus to wash him clean. *He* wanted to tell Jesus what to do. But Peter had it backward.

We may or may not be quite as impetuous as Peter, but I wonder, do we sometimes protest as he did? Do we sometimes have things backward, where we want to tell God what to do and how to do it? Do we expect a celebrity

Maundy Thursday

Savior instead of a servant Lord? By washing the feet of his disciples, Jesus challenged Peter and challenges all of us. "For the son of man came not to be served but to serve, and to give his life a ransom for many" (Mark 10:45).

We call on you as teacher and Lord, and just like Peter, we think we know what that means. But you go on to surprise us again and again. As Lord of all, you took the role of servant to wash your disciples' feet, to lay down your life for the world. Continue to teach us, continue to surprise us, as we follow in your way. Amen.

Good Friday
John 18:1-19:42

Facing Death

"That was a good funeral."
Before becoming a pastor, I wouldn't have understood what she meant, but now I could agree with this senior member of my church. We had just said goodbye to one of our dear saints who had been an active volunteer in the church and community until she had fallen ill, who had remained on good terms with all of her family who surrounded her with love and care, who had been a woman of prayer and faithful to the end. At her funeral, we sang some of her favorite songs, read words of comfort from scripture, heard wonderful family tributes, and shared food plus more stories after the service. It was a good funeral because of the life she had lived, the legacy of good relationships that she had left behind, and life eternal with no more sorrow or pain.
Just as she had a good funeral, she also had a good death. She had been well cared for in the hospice where church members, friends, and family could visit her at any time. When I stopped by to pray with her, she gave me a needlepoint that she had done, and showed me how she had tucked it into an envelope with my name on it, "in case I was gone before you came again," she said. She knew she was dying, and she faced death with faith for the future, with grace in her relationships with others, with the same creativity and generosity that she had demonstrated throughout her life.

The gospel of John tells the story of Jesus' good life followed by his good death and resurrection. Just as Jesus lived in submission to God, so he submitted to God's will in his suffering and death. He refused to fight to defend himself; instead, he told Peter to put away his sword, and he healed the high priest's slave whose ear had been cut off in his brief scuffle with Peter. Even while he suffered on the cross, he cared tenderly for his mother and arranged for her to live with one of his disciples. Jesus knew he was dying, and he faced death with the same care that he had always shown to others, with the same confidence in God that characterized his life and ministry.

In his suffering and death, Jesus certainly did not see himself as a victim. He was the victor! In fact, he often spoke of his death, resurrection, and ascension as "glorification." When he predicted his death, he said to his disciples, "The hour has come for the son of man to be glorified" (John 12:23). After he washed their feet, he again spoke of his death in similar terms: "Now the son of man is glorified and God is glorified in him" (John 13:31). When Jesus prayed for his disciples one last time before his arrest, he prayed, "Father, the hour has come. Glorify your son, that your son may glorify you" (John 17:1).

The gospel of John speaks of Jesus' death as an act of supreme agency where Jesus was not forced into dying on the cross or manipulated into giving up his life. Instead, he deliberately laid it down. "I lay down my life in order to take it up again," said Jesus. "No one takes it from me, but I lay it down of my own accord. I have power to lay it down, and I have power to take it up again. I have received this command from my Father" (John 10:17-18).

Our text for today shows Jesus in action, facing death head on, deliberately laying down his life just as he said. When Judas brought the authorities to the garden where

Good Friday

Jesus had gone with the rest of his disciples, Jesus did not try to hide from them or avoid them in any way; instead, the text says that "Jesus, knowing all that was to happen to him, came forward" (John 18:4). Jesus went forward to meet those who had come to arrest him. He went forward to meet suffering and death.

When the high priest questioned Jesus about his disciples and his teaching, their roles soon became reversed as Jesus went on to challenge the high priest. Jesus pointed out how he had always taught out in the open where the high priest or anyone could hear his teaching. He answered the high priest with a question of his own: "Why do you ask me?" (John 18:21). While the high priest seemed bent on interrogating Jesus, he found that Jesus began interrogating him.

When Jesus was taken to Pilate for further questioning, Jesus confronted him as well. To Pilate's first question, Jesus responded, "Do you ask this on your own, or did others tell you about me?" (John 18:34). His answer immediately put Pilate on the defensive, and their verbal sparring continued. When Pilate asked Jesus, "So you are a king?" Jesus replied, "You say that I am a king" (John 18:37). I can just imagine Pilate throwing up his hands in exasperation as he exclaimed, "What is truth?" (John 18:38). He knew he had no case against Jesus, and went to announce that to the crowds.

But the crowds would not listen, so Pilate returned to question Jesus once more. At first Jesus would not answer, and when he finally spoke, he only said, "You would have no power over me unless it had been given you from above" (John 19:11). With this challenge to his authority from Jesus, and with the shouts of the crowd ringing in his ears, Pilate finally turned Jesus over to suffer a humiliating and cruel death on the cross. Some of the soldiers even stole his clothes, divided them among themselves, and cast lots to see who would get the best piece. Jesus endured through all of the pain and abuse, until finally at the moment of his own choosing, he laid down his life. "It is finished," he said (John 29:30). His moment of glorification had come.

Jesus faced death with such fearlessness, with such a holy fierceness, that he went forward to meet those who had come to arrest him, he confronted and questioned the authorities, he laid down his life just as he had predicted. Just as he had spoken openly and boldly during his public ministry, when he spoke to the high priest and to Pilate, he again spoke openly and boldly.

The example of Jesus stands in stark contrast with the experience of Peter whose story of denial also forms part of our text. While Jesus faced the authorities boldly, Peter tried to hide his identity from the servants of the high priest who saw him in the courtyard. While Jesus questioned both the high priest and Pilate and put them on the defensive, Peter seemed defensive from the beginning, as one denial followed another until he had denied Jesus three times. After Jesus' resurrection, all would be forgiven, and Peter would one day glorify God in his death too (John 21:15-19), but at this point in the gospel narrative, Jesus' glorification takes center stage.

In this story, I would be Peter—curious and concerned enough about Jesus to follow him after his arrest, but fearful enough to follow only at a distance. I would want to be faithful as Peter insisted he would be, but my resolve would quite likely dissolve at the first question as Peter lost his resolve. I too would fail Jesus miserably. And maybe you would too.

Good Friday

But for Peter and for all of us, Jesus' death and resurrection mean forgiveness and new life. However miserably we might fail God, fail others, and fail ourselves, whatever sins we have committed, whatever failures, whatever regrets we may have about the past, Jesus' sacrifice and God's grace are greater.

That's why we dare to call this Good Friday. Because in spite of the injustice and brutality of Jesus' arrest, torture, and death, he died a "good" death—without fear under interrogation and torture; with more integrity than Pilate who condemned him to death even while he knew Jesus was innocent; confident of God's authority over every human authority; looking toward resurrection and new life. Jesus' good death proved to be good for us all.

O God of life and death, we are grateful for Good Friday, for Jesus who laid down his life. We are grateful that you are the God of resurrection, for Jesus raised from the dead by your power. We don't understand how Jesus could endure all that he went through. We don't understand the mystery of his resurrection. But by faith we receive your mercy, we receive your forgiveness, we receive new life. Amen.

Easter Sunday/Resurrection Of Our Lord
Matthew 28:1-10

Forgiven

Instead of making new year's resolutions, each year I like to choose a key word to help set my direction for the coming year. One year I chose "wonder," which for me meant being curious, exploring new things, and asking questions. It meant being filled with wonder at God's creation and work in the world and in my own life. That year it seemed as if the word had chosen me, for as soon as I settled on "wonder" as my word for the year, I started seeing wonder everywhere.

This year I chose "blossom," and when I asked friends what word they would choose for the coming year and why, I was amazed at the range of their answers: delight, trust, grace, victory, prayer, forgive, harmony, intentional, contemplation, longing, rich, letting go, and more. "I'm choosing letting go to remind myself that some burdens aren't mine to carry," said one. "My word is forgive because my friend needs it—to set my friend free and to set me free too," said another.

I've been thinking of those two comments ever since. They were made independently of one another in two separate conversations, but they go together in my mind. After all, the burden of sin is one burden that we don't need to carry, that we can let go, for Jesus' life, death, and resurrection conquered sin and death for us. That burden is now lifted. We are free! And the forgiveness and freedom we receive by faith in Jesus Christ are not for us alone. We can extend and receive forgiveness to and from one another also. We are set free, and they are too.

In our reading today, by the time Mary Magdalene and the other Mary arrived at the tomb, Jesus had already risen! Our text says, "suddenly there was a great earthquake; for an angel of the Lord, descending from heaven, came and rolled back the stone" (verse 2). I love this detail, for the tomb was already empty. The angel didn't roll back the stone to let Jesus out of the tomb. The angel rolled back the stone so the women - and later, the other disciples - could see in. They could see the place where Jesus' body had been. They could see the empty grave clothes. But Jesus himself was already gone.

"Do not be afraid," said the angel (verse 5). The guards had been so afraid when the angel appeared that they had all passed out. The women were so afraid that they could hardly wait for the angel to finish speaking, before they started running as fast as they could away from the tomb. Even though the angel said, do not be afraid, they were shaking with fear, and yet somehow filled with great relief and joy. Jesus had risen from the dead!

While the women were still on their way to find the rest of the disciples, Jesus himself suddenly appeared before them. Jesus greeted them with a customary form of address often translated as "greetings," but taken very literally, the word means "rejoice!" There may be a bit of a play on words here - for Jesus greeted them not only to say hello, but with an added note of celebration, "Rejoice!"

Easter Sunday / Resurrection Of The Lord

Then Jesus repeated the angel's message to the women with one significant change. "Do not be afraid," said the angel (verse 5). "Do not be afraid," said Jesus (verse 10). "[G]o quickly and tell his disciples," said the angel (verse 7). "[G]o and tell my brothers," said Jesus (verse 10).

Did you notice the difference? The women ran from the tomb to find the others—the men who had deserted Jesus in his moment of need, the ones who ran away when he was arrested, who denied even knowing him. For the angel to call them Jesus' disciples was already quite generous, for as disciples they had failed their teacher and Lord. But Jesus went even further for he called them "my brothers."

Even though his disciples had failed him miserably, Jesus reached out to them with this expression of grace, forgiveness, and reconciliation. That expression of undeserved grace was part of Jesus' Easter morning celebration, and part of his teaching throughout his ministry.

One day as Jesus was teaching, Peter had asked him, "How often should I forgive? As many as seven times?" Perhaps Peter thought he was being generous, but Jesus replied, "Not seven times, but, I tell you, seventy-seven times" (Matthew 18:21-22). Then Jesus went on to tell the story of an unforgiving servant whose master had forgiven his debts, yet the servant refused to forgive another servant who owed him money. When the master heard, he was furious and imprisoned the unforgiving servant until his entire debt would be repaid. The story ends with a stern warning to the disciples to forgive their brothers and sisters (Matthew 28:23-35).

That's exactly what Jesus does. On the cross, he had prayed for those who crucified him, and now in the power of his resurrection he extended forgiveness to those who had deserted and denied him. Instead of issuing a word of stern rebuke, Jesus tenderly called them "my brothers."

Today that same forgiveness can be ours in Jesus Christ. Whatever our past failures, whatever our present situation, in Jesus there is forgiveness from sin as he reaches out to call us sisters and brothers. There is freedom from the past. There is power to live a new life. And as we are forgiven, we in turn are called to forgive others.

That's how God celebrated Easter — by forgiving people who didn't deserve it, forgiving us even though we don't deserve it. That's how Jesus celebrated Easter, by forgiving those who deserted and denied him, by calling them my brothers and going to meet them.

You may or may not have a chosen a word for this year. But what if we were to make "forgiven" our word for Easter? What if we were to celebrate Easter by forgiving someone in our lives who doesn't deserve it? Can we go beyond the Easter egg hunt, the chocolates, the family gatherings, the wonderful Easter music and worship service to something more this year? In response to God's grace and forgiveness for us, can we also go on to forgive someone else in our lives?

That might mean forgiving the neighbor you find so irritating, or the co-worker you don't get along with. It might mean forgiving the church member who always disagrees with you or your sister or brother who bugs you. It might mean forgiving your father or mother, your friend, or your church family that wasn't there for you. It might even mean forgiving yourself for something you've done in the past and have never laid to rest.

Easter Sunday / Resurrection Of The Lord

Forgiveness doesn't mean condoning bad behavior or allowing it to continue. Forgiveness doesn't mean excusing or minimizing criminal or evil acts. But instead of holding the hurt inside where it can fester, forgiveness means we channel our pain and anger into making things right. We can release those hard feelings, have compassion on ourselves, and begin to have compassion on others. Instead of looking for revenge we can reach toward justice and reconciliation.

You probably didn't expect to work that hard on Easter Sunday. But Jesus' life, death, and resurrection means that we have forgiveness from sin and the power to live a new life — and that includes the power to forgive. This year, why not make forgiveness part of your Easter celebration? Receive the forgiveness of God through faith in Jesus Christ, and pass it on by forgiving someone who has wronged you - not because you agree with what they did - not because they deserve it, but because God in Jesus Christ has forgiven you. Be forgiven. Be free.

O God of resurrection and life, you transform death into life, you turn fear into joy, and you grant forgiveness from sin through faith in Jesus. As you bring forgiveness and new life into our lives, by your grace and power, may we also live out that good news. As forgiven people, may we also extend forgiveness to others. For the joy of the Lord gives wings to our feet to share the good news. Amen.

Easter 2

John 20:19-31

With Peace For The Fearful

In 1841, Edgar Allen Poe published one of the first locked-room murder mysteries, and since then many authors have offered variations on the theme. A single door stands locked from the inside, and must be forced open. The room has no chimney for escape to the roof, no false walls to a secret passage, no trap door. The only window remains bolted from the inside. Yet the poor man or woman lies dead on the floor, obviously the victim of foul play. In print, on stage and screen, a locked-room mystery centers on who did it, and how.

Our scripture reading for today presents another kind of locked-room mystery, although it predates the modern mystery novel by many centuries. The single door remains locked from the inside. The room has no false walls to a secret passage, no trap door. But instead of revealing a murder, this locked-room mystery goes in the opposite direction to show how Jesus' disciples move from fear to joy and new life!

Unlike most locked-room mysteries, this is no whodunit, for the text clearly tells us that Jesus entered that locked room. How did Jesus do it? Could he walk through walls like some superhero? Was he already in the locked room and simply revealed himself at the opportune time? The text seems quite unconcerned with such questions.

Instead of "whodunit" or even how he did it, the emphasis falls squarely on what happened when Jesus entered the locked room.

Just before Jesus appeared, our text tells us that the disciples were in the locked room "for fear of the Jews" (verse 19). Only a few days earlier, Jesus had been arrested, tortured, and executed. The disciples not only grieved the death of their teacher, but they couldn't help worrying whether they might be next to suffer a similar fate. Simon Peter had already denied knowing Jesus, fearing that he might be found guilty by association. Then the women had returned from the tomb with the strange story that Jesus had risen from the dead. Simon Peter and another disciple had seen the empty tomb for themselves. Mary Magdalene even claimed to have seen Jesus and talked with him.

These latest events simply added to their fears. Something very strange was going on. Something they could not explain. So in confusion and fear, they retreated together behind locked doors. At least there might be some safety in numbers, and they could share their grief and console one another.

Then suddenly they were not alone. "Jesus came and stood among them and said, 'Peace be with you'" (verse 19). I can imagine the sudden, jaw-dropping silence as the disciples tried to make sense of what they heard and saw in that moment. Was this really Jesus? Or was this a ghost? Were they all seeing and hearing things in a mass hallucination, or was this real? For a moment, their confusion and fear might have actually jumped a notch.

Yet the words "peace be with you" may have also sounded oddly reassuring. They had heard the traditional greeting many times before and had repeated it many times themselves. It was the kind of greeting you might offer to an extended family member you hadn't seen for a while, or to a neighbor you might meet on the way to the temple. And here was their dear friend--the one who had been crucified and buried - greeting them in the traditional way as if it were the most normal thing in the world. Would a ghost or a mass hallucination behave like that?

In that moment, the disciples might have also heard the echo of Jesus' words shortly before his death: "Peace I leave with you; my peace I give to you. I do not give to you as the world gives. Do not let your hearts be troubled, and do not let them be afraid." (John 14:27). Now here, as the resurrected Jesus appeared to them, he once again spoke a word of peace. No word of rebuke. No "don't you remember what I told you earlier about my death and resurrection?" "Peace be with you." Instead of being fearful, the disciples could now be at peace because Jesus was with them once again.

What a mystery! Jesus appeared to the disciples even though they were meeting behind locked doors. He still bore the scars where his hands had been nailed to the cross, where his side had been pierced by a soldier's sword to make sure that he was dead. How could this be? The disciples themselves were still confused, but they got the main point: Jesus had truly risen from the dead! When the disciples realized that Jesus was once again fully alive before them, their fear turned to great joy.

In our text, the disciples' transformation from fear to joy takes just two verses, from verse 19 to verse 20. When I read that far, I wanted to stop. Those two verses contained more than enough for one sermon, or even a series of sermons. From fear to joy, from mourning the death of Jesus to delighting in his presence, from cowering behind locked doors to finding peace - that was already more than enough for the disciples and for us today - or so I thought.

But the text doesn't allow us to stop reading after those two verses. Instead, the next verse continues with Jesus repeating his greeting, "Peace be with you" (verse 21). It's as if the disciples had gotten so excited by his appearance that they all started talking at the same time, so Jesus needed to quiet them down to listen once more. The repeated greeting meant that Jesus had not yet finished. He had a further message for them: "As the Father has sent me, so I send you" (verse 21).

The disciples were not meant to stay in that locked room celebrating their newfound joy and peace in the resurrected Jesus. Their restored relationship with the Lord was not only for them as individuals or as a small group. It was meant for all those crouched in fear behind locked doors, for all those just as confused and upset, for all those who had not yet heard, seen, and believed that death was not the end. As Jesus himself had entered the disciples' locked room with a word of peace, so he also commissioned them with the same message.

Just as Edgar Allen Poe's locked-room mystery has been repeated with many variations over the years, so this mystery of Jesus entering the locked rooms of human life has also been repeated many times. A week later, the disciples were again together in the same place, and this time Thomas was also with them. Again the doors were shut, and again Jesus suddenly appeared to them. Again he greeted them with the words, "Peace be with you" (verse 21). Just as Jesus had earlier shown his scars to the other disciples, he showed them again to Thomas, and he too immediately believed.

Today that same mystery of the locked room can be replayed in our own lives as well. Like Thomas and the other disciples, we each have our own fears—fears of what other people might do or say, fears for our safety or the safety of our family. We have our own doubts, our own insecurities that keep us locked behind closed doors. But just as he did so long ago, Jesus can enter our locked rooms with new life and a word of peace. He sets us free and sends us out in joy.

> *When Jesus appeared to Thomas and showed him his scars, Thomas cried out, "My Lord and my God!" So we cry out to you, "My Lord and my God": deliver us from the locked rooms of fear, uncertainty, and doubt. Transform us by your joy and peace that we may live with trust and confidence in you. Then send us as your disciples to be faithful witnesses of your life and power. Amen.*

Easter 3

Luke 24:13-35

With Burning Hearts

My father-in-law loved to do jigsaw puzzles, and would always begin by separating the pieces according to color. He worked on a large surface, so he had room to spread out, with all of the blue pieces in one pile, all of the red pieces in another pile, all of the dark pieces together, and so on. For this initial sorting, he wasn't concerned whether a blue piece was part of the sky or part of the water, or if a dark piece was part of a tree trunk or the side of a barn. Those finer distinctions would come later as he went on to put the puzzle together.

As he worked, he would sometimes carefully examine a single puzzle piece and hold it up to the completed picture on the box, until that aha! moment where he would find its exact spot. Suddenly he could see that the bit of blue was indeed water and the darker part of the puzzle piece part of the river bank.

My father-in-law's puzzle-solving method has never worked for me. Separating all of the colors first seems like a slow way to start, so I generally look for all of the straight edges first, build the frame, and then fill in the rest of the puzzle pieces from there. For more of a challenge, I most often do this without referring to the picture on the box. Yes, I might know in general terms that the finished scene would be a landscape, or the Golden Gate Bridge, or something else, but that would be enough for me. Just as

I don't have the patience to sort hundreds of pieces into colors, I don't have the patience to scrutinize the picture to find just the right spot for a single puzzle piece. By trial and error, I eventually figure it out.

As two of Jesus' disciples travelled on the road from Jerusalem to Emmaus, their conversation centered on everything that had happened in the last number of days. We might say they were puzzling over all that had happened. They seemed to have all of the facts—all of the pieces of the puzzle—but they didn't yet know the significance of each one and hadn't yet been able to put all of the pieces together so they made sense. They didn't yet have the complete picture.

They knew that Jesus had been a prophet who found favor with God and with the people. They knew that he had been arrested and put to death. They even knew that Jesus' body was missing. When they were joined by a stranger on the road, they freely related all of these facts. They couldn't dismiss these things that they had heard, but they couldn't quite put all of the pieces together and understand that Jesus had been raised from the dead. Instead of being overcome with joy that Jesus had risen, they were sad.

Perhaps their grief was part of the reason that they were not able to recognize Jesus. As far as they knew, this stranger was just another one of the many travelers on the road from Jerusalem to Emmaus. Strangers traveling alone would often attach themselves to groups for greater safety, so perhaps it was no surprise to have a stranger join their conversation. The two disciples told him their sad story and how they had hoped Jesus would redeem Israel, but with his death, their hopes had been crushed.

Jesus was quick to respond: "Oh, how foolish you are, and how slow of heart to believe all that the prophets have declared! Was it not necessary that the Messiah should suffer these things and then enter into his glory?" (verses 25-26). Then Jesus explained the Scriptures to them. Quite likely, they had heard the words of the prophets many times before. But this time, they heard them in relation to Jesus' own suffering and death.

Perhaps Jesus drew their attention to the prophet Isaiah who foretold his death for the forgiveness of sin: "But he was wounded for our transgressions, crushed for our iniquities; upon him was the punishment that made us whole, and by his bruises we are healed" (Isaiah 53:5). Or perhaps he pointed them to the Psalms which he quoted even on the cross: "My God, my God, why have you forsaken me?" (Psalm 22:1). Or to the prophet Zechariah who foretold his triumphal entry into Jerusalem the week before his death: "Rejoice greatly, O daughter Zion! Shout aloud, O daughter Jerusalem! Lo, your king comes to you; triumphant and victorious is he, humble and riding on a donkey, on a colt, the foal of a donkey" (Zechariah 9:9).

When they arrived at the village of Emmaus, Jesus walked ahead as if he meant to travel further. But it was almost evening, and traveling alone at night was even more of a safety issue, so Cleopas and his companion urged Jesus to stay with them. Then at the table, Jesus took the bread, blessed it, broke it, and that's when they finally recognized who he was!

For the two disciples, the facts of the story were still the same as they had earlier described them. Really nothing had changed - everything that had happened was exactly the same. And yet, everything was different! For in hearing the words of scripture, and breaking bread with

Jesus, they could finally put the pieces together. The empty tomb meant that Jesus had risen! They could hope again in Jesus as their redeemer! No religious authority, political power, or death sentence could keep him down. Jesus had won the victory over sin and death. Their crucified Lord was living and present with them. Instead of shock and sadness over all that had happened, instead of confusion, the disciples could rejoice!

The two disciples were now so excited that they hurried back to Jerusalem, even though it was already evening and not the best time for traveling, even though it was seven miles between Emmaus and Jerusalem. This couldn't wait until morning - they had to get back. They had to tell the others. The good news of Jesus' resurrection and living presence was not just a personal, inner belief. It was meant to be lived out. It was meant to be shared. And so they hurried to Jerusalem.

When they arrived, they found the other disciples just as excited about the good news - while the two of them had been on the road between Emmaus and Jerusalem, the risen Lord had also appeared to Simon. This very strange story wasn't fake news. It was confirmed in the testimony of the women who had seen the angel, in the witness of Peter and John who had run to the empty tomb, in the reports of Mary Magdalene and Simon Peter who had both seen the risen Lord, and in their own experience as well.

This is one of my favorite Easter stories, in part because it's about two relatively unknown disciples of Jesus. The name of Cleopas appears nowhere else in scripture, and the other disciple remains unnamed in our text. Some have suggested that the unidentified disciple may have been the wife of Cleopas, that she and her husband actually lived in Emmaus, and that it was into their own home that they invited Jesus.

These were ordinary disciples of Jesus - people who believed in him, but who could also be confused about events in the world around them; people who had hopes that could be shattered; people who weren't able to recognize Jesus even when he walked beside them; people who needed to understand scripture, who needed to meet Jesus in the breaking of bread. In other words, they were ordinary people just like you and me.

Like the two disciples on the road to Emmaus, many of us are also very familiar with the facts of Jesus' life, death, and resurrection. But beyond the basic facts of Easter, can we also see their significance for ourselves as ordinary disciples today? Will our eyes be opened so we will see Jesus alive and victorious over sin and death? Will our hearts burn within us? Will we be so transformed that we'll change the direction of our lives?

That's what Easter meant to the two disciples on the road to Emmaus, and that's what Easter can mean for us today as well. If you're confused by the things going on in the world or in your own life, please know that the crucified and risen Christ walks with you. If you have some broken dreams, some disappointments that make you stand still and feel sad, please know that the crucified and risen Christ can bring new purpose and meaning to your life. If you're going your own way, you can change direction and come to Jesus. Whatever we face in life or in death, Jesus has already won the victory. There is life abundant and life eternal through faith in him.

On The Way With Jesus

O crucified and risen Christ, when our way is confusing, sad, or joyous, open our eyes to your presence, make our hearts burn within us, and lead us to an ever deeper understanding of your life, death, and resurrection. Amen.

Easter 4

John 10:1-10

With Challenge And Invitation

Jesus loved to tell stories. In his preaching and teaching, a man traveling on the road became the focal point in a lesson on being a good neighbor. A wayward son welcomed home by his father taught a lesson about God's love and forgiveness. Over and over, Jesus used vivid images to express his own identity: I am the light of the world. I am the true vine. I am the Bread of Life.

In our scripture reading for today, Jesus told another story to communicate his identity and mission. Shepherds and sheep would have been common sights in his ancient rural setting. His listeners would have understood how sheep would be gathered into a sheepfold for safety overnight. The gate would be closed with the shepherd stationed at the entrance. A thief might possibly try to climb over the fence, but if the sheep were disturbed, they would only mill about and try to get away from the stranger. Only the shepherd could open and close the gate, and when he called the sheep, they would respond to his familiar voice and follow him.

Our text calls this story a "figure of speech," a proverb or parable with a symbolic meaning. In this case, the parable speaks of Jesus as both shepherd and gatekeeper, and his followers as the sheep that belong to him. Jesus makes this clear just after our reading, where he says, "I am the Good Shepherd. The Good Shepherd lays down his life for the sheep" (John 10:11).

Jesus also said, "I am the gate"; in fact he says it twice (verses 7, 9). To our twenty-first-century ears, it may seem confusing for Jesus to be the Good Shepherd, the gatekeeper, and the gate all at the same time. But his manner of speaking is similar when he later talked with his disciples about "the way" he is going, and then says, "I am the way" (John 14:4, 6). It's as if no one image is enough to describe who Jesus is: light, water, bread, vine, shepherd, gatekeeper, gate, way, and more. Each image conveys part of who Jesus is - who God is - and no one image is enough.

These ten verses from the gospel of John are part of that wonderful collage. They form a beautifully rich parable of God as the shepherd who cares for the sheep night and day, who keeps them safe like the gate of the sheepfold, and protects them from anyone who might try to harm them or steal them away. Jesus' disciples and all of us are the sheep who belong to him, who gather together, who listen for his voice. As a parable of our relationship with God, this word picture paints a warm and tender portrait.

However, in the context of the gospel of John, this parable also functions as Jesus' commentary on his healing of a man who had been blind from birth. These ten verses appear at the start of chapter ten, and the chapter break might suggest that this is the start of a new subject. But at the end of chapter nine, Jesus was still speaking with the man who was now able to see. "I came into this world for judgment so that those who do not see may see, and those who do see may become blind," says Jesus (John 9:39). Some of the Pharisees protested, for Jesus' words seemed to be aimed at them, and their conversation then continued into chapter ten with Jesus' response.

This reveals Jesus' parable as something much more than a tender portrait of God's care. Instead of a stand-alone story, it's a continuation of the Pharisees' dispute with Jesus. They had already questioned the man who had miraculously received his sight. They had questioned his parents to confirm that their son had actually been born blind. Then they questioned the man again, and when they were not satisfied with his answers, they put him out of the synagogue.

In the course of their investigation, the Pharisees seemed bent on discrediting Jesus. Some bluntly said, "This man is not from God, for he does not observe the sabbath" (John 9:16). Some said, "We know that this man is a sinner'" (John 9:24). Others added to the confusion and insisted, "We know that God has spoken to Moses, but as for this man, we do not know where he comes from." (John 9:29).

As a master storyteller, Jesus answered their concerns with this story. No, he was not some unknown stranger - he was the shepherd and gatekeeper for the sheep. Just as a shepherd would look after the welfare of his sheep, Jesus had looked after the welfare of the man who had been born blind. Instead of leaving him as a beggar at the side of the road, Jesus had given him the gift of sight both physically and spiritually. The man received his physical eyesight once he had washed in the pool of Siloam, and then his spiritual sight developed as he came to know Jesus as healer, prophet, and finally as Lord.

No, Jesus was not a sinner. He was the Good Shepherd. Like the shepherd of Psalm 23, Jesus provided for the needs of his sheep, in this case by restoring the sight of the man who had been born blind. Jesus blessed him with goodness and mercy, and the man blessed Jesus by his worship.

But Jesus' portrayal of himself as the Good Shepherd also had an edge to it. In the prophetic writings of the Jewish people, the leaders were often referred to as shepherds, and often in unflattering terms. So the prophet Jeremiah said, "For the shepherds are stupid, and do not inquire of the Lord; therefore they have not prospered, and all their flock is scattered" (Jeremiah 10:21). The prophet Ezekiel described the leaders of the people as shepherds more concerned with feeding themselves than feeding their sheep. He announced to them this word of the Lord: "You have not strengthened the weak, you have not healed the sick, you have not bound up the injured, you have not brought back the strayed, you have not sought the lost, but with force and harshness you have ruled them" (Ezekiel 34:4).

This prophetic background would have been familiar to the Pharisees, and as leaders of the people, they must have felt Jesus' words directed at them. If Jesus was the good shepherd, did he mean then to cast the Pharisees as the stupid shepherds? Did he mean to proclaim judgment on them? After all, Jesus had healed the man of his blindness, and they had put the man out of the synagogue. At the end of their encounter with Jesus, some of the Pharisees were still divided between dismissing his words and being convicted by them (John 10:19-21).

Today Jesus' words present a challenge and invitation to all of us. To all of us as leaders - as parents, as church members, in our work life, wherever we exercise influence, wherever our actions impact other people - are we good shepherds or bandits? In other words, do we seek the health and well-being of those placed in our care, or do we do harm? Are we wise shepherds who seek God's will and way, or are we stupid shepherds who act in our own self-interest? To all of us as sheep, Jesus invites us to enter by the gate and find abundant life. Do we hear and recognize his voice? Will we listen? The good shepherd is calling.

Convict us, Lord, to be leaders who do what is right, who serve with integrity, who look to heal instead of harm, who bind up wounds instead of making them worse, who encourage the weak instead of trampling over them, and who protect instead of tearing down. As people who belong to you, make us eager to listen for your voice and eager to follow. Like the blind man whose eyes were opened physically and spiritually, may we also know your abundant life. Amen.

Easter 5

John 14:1-14

The Way For Troubled Hearts

A young mother said that she was worried about the kind of world her children were growing up in. When her own mother was a child, her mother walked by herself to school; now, like all of the other parents she knows, this young mom always drives her children. New technologies at school and home seem to bring new pressures and new problems. In her nice suburban neighborhood, there was a stabbing in a nearby high school that left one student dead and another seriously injured.

Concerned mothers like her are understandably troubled. Even when there is much to celebrate on Mother's Day and at other times of the year, there may also be that undercurrent of uncertainty and anxiety. What is happening in the world around us? What will the future bring? What will become of us, and our children and grandchildren, and future generations?

It's not only young mothers who may be anxious and troubled today. There seems to be enough anxiety going around for everyone: worries related to family stress, parenting challenges and parenting our parents, physical and mental illness, homelessness, racism, human rights violations, political corruption and unrest, church conflict, struggles at work, unresolved relationships, finances, and more. No wonder some say that anxiety is the disease of the twenty-first century! But anxiety has been around a lot longer than that.

In our reading today, Jesus' disciples had good reason to be anxious. Our text formed part of Jesus' farewell speech to his disciples after their last supper together and before Jesus would be arrested, put on trial, and crucified. Jesus had just given them three pieces of disturbing news: 1) he would be leaving, and they wouldn't be able to come with him; 2) one of them would betray him; and 3) Peter would deny him.

How could any of that possibly be? The disciples had left home, family, and livelihood to follow Jesus, and he was saying they would no longer be able to follow him. They were Jesus' closest friends and followers. They had returned with him to Jerusalem in spite of the growing opposition against him and at the risk of their own safety. How could Jesus possibly say that one of them would betray him? When others had turned away, and Jesus asked whether the disciples would also leave, Peter had answered for the group: "Lord, to whom can we go? You have the words of eternal life" (John 6:68). After that declaration, how could he possibly think that Peter would deny him? Jesus' words must have confused and worried his disciples.

That's when he said, "Do not let your hearts be troubled" (verse 1a). Are you kidding, Jesus? How were they to stop? How are we to stop? How are we to stop being nervous or stop being anxious? Just stop. But Jesus was totally serious, and in the next breath, he gave his alternative to worry: "Believe in God, believe also in me" (verse 1b).

The word "believe" may suggest an intellectual exercise. We believe with our minds. But at a deeper level, belief is not only about what we think. Belief resides not only in our heads, but in our hearts. In the Bible, the heart isn't simply the physical heart muscle that keeps beating and keeps us alive. The heart stands for the entire person - our mind, emotions, and total being. To convey this larger sense of believing with our whole selves, we might say, "Trust in God, trust also in me."

Trust is not a one-time action. It's an ongoing relationship. It's part belief in our heads, and it's also belief in our hearts, belief expressed by the way we live. Trust means committing our whole being to God. So God's peace for troubled hearts is for the entire person - our troubled thoughts, our troubled feelings, our troubled everything.

The French poet and author, Victor Hugo, is perhaps most well-known for his novels, *The Hunchback of Notre Dame* and *Les Miserables*. This quote is often attributed to him as well: "Have courage for the great sorrows of life and patience for the small ones; and when you have laboriously accomplished your daily task, go to sleep in peace. God is awake." With these words, he paints a picture of what it means to trust God.

Trusting God does not mean that our troubles disappear. Trusting God does not mean that life will always be calm. We may well be in the midst of a storm of events that make us anxious. But trusting God means having courage for the great sorrows we face in living and in dying. Not because those things don't matter, but because no matter how heavy the burden, God is with us and at work. Trust means having patience for the small things: when you have to wait for test results, or there's a traffic jam, or you have to make a second trip to the store because you forgot to buy the milk. God is with us and at work at those times too.

At the same time, trusting God does not absolve us of all responsibility. In fact when we're troubled about something, that may well point to where we need to work, where we need to pray. So if we're troubled about our children's school, trusting God may mean we need to volunteer. If we're troubled by safety issues in our community, trusting God may mean building community by welcoming newcomers, getting to know our neighbors, and building healthy relationships. If we're troubled by mental illness, trusting God may mean seeking counseling or taking medication and learning to rest.

Some of this may be laborious work. Like Jesus' disciples, we may not always know the way forward. "How can we know the way?" asked Thomas (verse 5). And Philip too seemed uncertain, for he said to Jesus, "Lord, show us the Father," as if he didn't yet know that God was with him (verse 8). At least they knew to go to Jesus with their questions, and we can too.

Trusting God means realizing the limits of our knowledge, the limits of our wisdom, as well as the limits of our time and energy. We're not actually responsible for everything. We don't need to run ourselves into the ground. There is a God who is sovereign, who knows all, who is awake, who is at work, and that God is not us.

When Jesus spoke God's peace to the troubled hearts of his disciples, he addressed them as a group. They were in shock over the announcement of his coming departure and what he said about their coming betrayal and denial. But they weren't alone. When Jesus said, "Do not let your hearts be troubled," he used the plural forms. "You" is the plural form. "Hearts" is plural. Jesus' words were personal, but they were not directed to the disciples as individuals. Instead, Jesus addressed them together as a group.

Easter 5

As a church, we also form a group of Jesus' disciples, and we can think of his words to us as a group. Whatever our anxieties might be - we might be anxious about our personal lives, we might be anxious about our life together as a church, we might be anxious about the world at large - we're not alone with our anxieties. We have God, and we have one another. Together, we can stop letting our hearts be troubled. Together we can trust in God.

This is the way of Jesus: the way of trust, the way of faith, the way of peace. It is the way for mothers on Mother's Day and all year round. It is the way for all of us whatever our circumstances. In our worship, we say that we believe in God - in the songs we sing, in the words of affirmation and confession that we repeat, and in the prayers we offer up each week. May that belief take deep root within us, so we might trust God with all of our heart and soul and mind and strength.

In times of trouble, we seek your refuge, O God of peace. In times of uncertainty, we seek your way forward. At all times, teach us to seek your presence, and place our trust in you. Amen.

Easter 6

John 14:15-21

Framed By Love

On my writing desk at home, I have a framed photo of my husband taken a number of years ago. It's a simple head and shoulders pose on a plain background in a slender gold-toned frame from a drug store. In other words, objectively speaking, the photo and its frame are really nothing special. They have no particular artistic or monetary value in the marketplace. Yet no matter how full my desk gets with books and files, papers and more papers, there's always room for that photo too, because I think of it as framed by love - the romantic love as husband and wife, the friendship and partnership love that has deepened over the years, the love we have for God who has joined us together.

The words of Jesus in our text this morning are also framed by love. At the start of our reading, he says, "If you love me, you will keep my commandments" (verse 15). This is no threat. Jesus is not saying, do this or else. Instead his words are a statement of identity. If you love me, this is how you will live. If you love me, you will keep my commandments. Then at the end of our reading, Jesus rephrases the same statement of identity: "They who have my commandments and keep them are those who love me" (verse 21).

Earlier in John's gospel, Jesus said to his disciples, "I give you a new commandment, that you love one another" (John 13:34). At the time, Jesus had just demonstrated his love for his disciples by washing their feet. For their teacher and Lord to perform such a lowly task for them was a striking illustration of his love and service. The "new commandment" was a reminder that they too were called to love one another.

Yet this so-called new commandment to love was already an old commandment, an ancient commandment. Centuries earlier in the Old Testament, God instructed the people, "You shall not take vengeance or bear a grudge against any of your people, but you shall love your neighbor as yourself: I am the Lord" (Leviticus 19:18). Earlier in Jesus' own ministry, when a lawyer asked him about the greatest commandment, Jesus spoke of loving God and loving your neighbor as yourself (Matthew 22:34-40; Mark 12:28-31, Luke 10:25-28).

So when Jesus told his disciples to love one another, he was hardly telling them anything new. Instead, he gave them a very old and very familiar commandment. They had heard it before and could probably say if off by heart. But the way Jesus defined love was new, for he said, "Just as I have loved you, you also should love one another" (John 13:34).

In his life and ministry, Jesus showed love for his disciples over and over again. He invited them into relationship with him. He shared the good news of God's kingdom and taught them. He settled their quarrels and answered their questions. He included them in his ministry. He would forgive them for falling asleep on him and deserting him in his time of need. And finally he would give up his life on the cross. Clearly for Jesus, love meant even more than washing feet.

Jesus' love for his disciples and for the world cost him his life. It was a self-giving, sacrificial love. It was love in action - often unexpected like washing feet or talking with a Samaritan woman or healing a blind man. For Jesus, love was literally a matter of life and death. What's more, Jesus said, that's how all people will know that you are my disciples, when you love one another just as I have loved you.

That's an impossibly high standard, isn't it? Who among the disciples could love like Jesus? Who among us can love in that surprising, self-giving, and sacrificial way? If that's the gold standard of love, we might as well cut our losses and give up now!

But in our text, Jesus also tells his disciples that he will not abandon them to struggle along on their own. Instead he says, "I will ask the Father, and he will give you another advocate, to be with you forever" (verse 16). The word "advocate" may also be translated as encourager, comforter, helper, mediator. Although Jesus would leave the disciples, God's Spirit as advocate and mediator would be ever present to encourage, comfort, and help them. That included helping the disciples to love one another.

For us today, God's Spirit also helps us. When love seems too demanding, when we struggle to live out our true identity as beloved by God and loving others, we have an encourager and helper. When we lose our way and need to find it again, we have an advocate and mediator to comfort us and bring us home.

When it comes to loving relationships today, many of us might think first of our biological families: mother and father, brother and sister, our spouse, our children. But Jesus himself remained single, and in his earthly ministry he expanded the definition of love and family life beyond the biological family. So when Jesus' mother and his siblings came looking for him, the gospel of Mark says that Jesus replied, "'Who are my mother and my brothers?' And looking at those who sat around him, he said, 'Here are my mother and my brothers! Whoever does the will of God is my brother and sister and mother'" (Mark 3:33-35). Jesus' definition of love and family reached beyond his biological family to include the family of faith.

As followers of Jesus, we also need to expand our definition of love and family to include the family of faith. That means our church family, and beyond that, the followers of Jesus in other congregations and denominations. Beyond the family of faith is the whole human family. In sending Jesus, God's love embraced the world. That's the kind of love Jesus showed in his life and death, and the kind of love God wants to work in and through us.

So what if we could frame everything that happens in our lives with love? What would that look like? If there's a family tragedy or some other difficulty among us, can we frame that with love by our prayers, by a visit, a hug, a card, a phone call or text or email, a casserole dish, some baking, dropping by with groceries, giving a ride, offering to care for the children, being quiet together, crying together.

What about when we disappoint and fail one another? If the definition of love is Jesus, then failure seems inevitable, and can we frame that with love? When we fall short, when we are too weary or pre-occupied to love others, can we confess and repent, make amends and forgive, and learn to care for one another again? Can we turn to God's Spirit to help us to keep loving one another?

And what about on a national and international scale? Instead of focusing only on our own needs, can we in love consider the needs of others? Can we demonstrate love by

Easter 6

acting with justice and mercy, by sharing what we have and not taking more? Instead of hostility, can our political debates and discussions be framed by words of love and kindness?

To make a start on any of this, we'll need to encourage one another, and we'll need to be reminded of Jesus' example and teaching. Our Lord leads the way. Our divine encourager helps us. So let us walk in the new commandment of Jesus, and love one another.

> *Our lives are framed by the love of God, from creation to new creation, from birth to life eternal. If we love him - since we love him - let us also love one another. With praise and thanks to God, Amen.*

Easter 7

John 17:1-11

Praying All The Way

If you could ask Jesus to pray for you, what would be your prayer request?

One on-line prayer wall invites anyone to pray and lists the following requests:

- Please pray for jc and lb. They need to communicate and have forgiveness.
- Direction for my family, mental health completely restored, protection for my son, and direction for a job where God wants me to serve.
- Please pray that my mom gets better and gets out of her wheelchair soon, and she gets her mind back, and starts to remember who we all are.
- Prayer is needed in my marriage, household, children, family, and all around.
- Pray for me and my recovery from drinking alcohol.

We don't know the individuals who posted these prayer requests. We don't have any background information or context to help us understand what they're asking. Perhaps their situations have changed by now, and their prayer requests might be quite different. But these represent the kinds of prayers that people ask for, the prayers that we might want to offer for ourselves or for people we know. So let's take a moment to pray for the needs that we're aware of in our own lives and the lives of those around us. (pause for prayer)

Scripture tells us that when we don't know how to pray, God's Spirit prays on our behalf: "Likewise the Spirit helps us in our weakness; for we do not know how to pray as we ought, but that very Spirit intercedes with sighs too deep for words" (Romans 8:26). At times we might well need those "sighs too deep for words." We may not know how to pray for the people and things that concern us. We may not even know what we need to pray for. But the Spirit knows and intercedes for us.

After Jesus' last supper with his disciples, and just before our text for today, Jesus encouraged his disciples to make their requests known to God: "Very truly, I tell you, if you ask anything of the Father in my name, he will give it to you. Until now you have not asked for anything in my name. Ask and you will receive, so that your joy may be complete" (John 16:23-24). What an offer! Just ask and you will receive. It's an offer that Jesus repeated several times in his farewell to his disciples. But they didn't respond, for all of their attention was taken up with the thought of Jesus' departure. They could hardly think of anything else. Instead, Jesus offered his own prayer that is sometimes referred to as his "high priestly prayer."

In the tradition of the Jewish people, the high priest was their representative who would enter the innermost part of the temple once a year to offer a sacrifice for the sins of the people. On the eve of Jesus' sacrifice, Jesus was the high priest who offered this prayer on behalf of his disciples. The prayer takes up all of John 17, and is the longest recorded prayer by Jesus in the gospels.

The first part of Jesus' prayer centered on God's glory. We might think of fireworks or a laser light show, a glittery ballroom and royalty, or the Academy Awards or a Nobel Prize. But the glory Jesus spoke of was the glory of finishing God's work, the glory of being in God's presence, the glory of returning to God by Jesus' own death on the cross. It was a rather gruesome glory, but that's what Jesus meant by glorifying God.

The second part of Jesus' prayer centered on his disciples. As far as we know, this was not the prayer they asked for, but the prayer that Jesus chose for them and chose for all of us as his followers. Jesus prayed for those who received his words and who believed in him sent from the Father. He prayed for those who belong to God--we might say for those who were part of the family of faith. Not because they or we asked for this prayer, but because Jesus was moved to pray as he prepared to leave this earth.

In his prayer, Jesus' two big requests were for protection and unity. He knew only too well the challenges of living in the world. He had faced plenty of criticism from those who opposed him and misunderstanding even from his closest friends and followers. He was about to be arrested, tried, and executed. Yet in spite of the tremendous costs, he remained steadfast in doing the work of his Father. For whatever challenges his disciples would face in the world - whatever criticism or misunderstanding or persecution - he prayed that God would protect them from losing their way (verses 12-15).

Jesus prayed for protection "so that" the disciples might know the same kind of unity that Jesus knew with his Father. The disciples had already been arguing among themselves about which one of them was the greatest

(Mark 9:33-34). James and John had already asked Jesus if they could sit next to him "in glory," at his immediate right and left in what they thought would be the best seats (Mark 10:35-41). Their mother had joined in their request, and the other disciples had been angry that they would ask Jesus for special favor (Matthew 20:20-24). Even then they needed protection from division and disunity.

We need that protection today too. As Christians, we are part of the body of Christ, part of a long line of believers that stretches all the way back to the first disciples of Jesus and that stretches into the future. We have a unity that crosses centuries and that crosses generations and geography; one that transcends class and culture; one that transcends denominational and congregational distinctives.

Yet in some ways, just like Jesus' first disciples, we're still arguing about who among us is the greatest. We're still struggling with family and church family dynamics that intensify our differences. We're still getting angry over issues that divide us. Jesus' prayer has not yet been fully answered.

Why not? Jesus prayed over fish and bread, and everyone in the crowd received their fill. He prayed at the tomb of Lazarus, and Lazarus was raised from the dead. But what happened when Jesus prayed for protection and unity for his disciples? One of them betrayed him and later died by suicide. Another denied him. All would end up deserting him. Today the church continues to fragment, and even individual congregations may have trouble staying together.

When it comes to Christian unity, we're clearly still living in the already-but-not-yet. If Jesus were here in the flesh to pray with us, he might still pray that same prayer for our protection and unity. Perhaps that's one of the prayers the Spirit still sighs over today.

Yet for Jesus' first disciples and for us, there are foretastes of that unity he prayed for. The disciples were gathered together when Jesus appeared to them after his resurrection. They received his great commission to share the good news, and the impact of their combined ministry has endured over the centuries. Today in my area, two churches of different denominations share the same building and partner together on community outreach. Two members in my congregation left a church meeting on a controversial subject, and one member put her arm around the other's shoulders and said, "We don't agree, but I love you."

As a church and as individuals and households, we're still on the way with Jesus. His prayer hasn't been fully answered yet, but God's not done with us yet either. So let us not grow weary and lose heart. Let's keep walking together and praying all the way.

O Father, Son, and Spirit, the triune God, we give you glory as creator, redeemer, and sustainer, the one who saves and sends us. We give thanks for our faith and fellowship. Protect us from division that mars our witness. Enlarge our unity and love for one another. Amen.

About The Author

April Yamasaki writes on spiritual growth and Christian living both online and in print publications. She is an ordained minister with 25 years of experience in pastoral ministry, and speaks widely in churches and other ministry settings. Her books include *Sacred Pauses: Spiritual Practices for Personal Renewal* and *Four Gifts: Seeking Self-Care for Heart, Soul, Mind, and Strength*. She currently serves as Resident Author with Valley CrossWay Church, which is a liturgical worship community, and is the Editor of *Purpose*, a monthly magazine of everyday inspiration. For more information, please visit her websites, aprilyamasaki.com and WhenYouWorkfortheChurch.com.